COMPARING ANIMAL TRAITS

AMERICAN ALLIGATORS

ARMORED ROARING REPTILES

REBECCA E. HIRSCH

Lerner Publications ◆ Minneapolis

Lerner Publications Company
A division of Lerner Publishing Group, Inc.
241 First Avenue North
Minneapolis, MN 55401 USA

For reading levels and more information, look up this title at www.lernerbooks.com.

Photo Acknowledgments

The images in this book are used with the permission of: © A. & J. Visage/Photolibrary/Getty Images, p. 1; © iStockphoto.com/ekratzig, p. 4; © iStockphoto.com/NNehring Alligator, p. 5; © Raffaella Calzoni/ Shutterstock.com, p. 6; © Joe McDonald/CORBIS, p. 7; © Sabena Jane Blackbird/Alamy, p. 8 (right); © Ekaterina Pokrovsky/Shutterstock.com, p. 8 (left); © iStockphoto.com/Dougfir, p. 9 (left); © iStockphoto. com/Snowleopard1, p. 9 (right); © David M. Dennis/Animals Animals, p. 10; James Carmichael Jr/NHPA/ Photoshot/Newscom, p. 11 (top); © Patrick K. Campbell/Shutterstock.com, p. 11 (bottom); © Laura Westlund/Independent Picture Service, p. 12; © chloe7992/Shutterstock.com, p. 13 (top); © Tim Chapman/ Hulton Archive/Getty Images, p. 13 (bottom); © Gerard Lacz/Animals Animals, p. 14; Evolve/Photoshot/ ZUMAPRESS/Newscom, p. 15 (top); © McDonald Wildlife Photography/Animals Animals, p. 15 (bottom); © Gary Nafis, p. 16; © iStockphoto.com/passion4nature, p. 17 (left); © Zigmund Leszczynski/Animals Animals, p. 17 (right); © Arto Hakola/Shutterstock.com, p. 18; © FloridaStock/Shutterstock.com, p. 19; © IndiaPictures/UIG via Getty Images, p. 20; © Minden Pictures/SuperStock, p. 21 (left); © iStockphoto. com/Gaschwald, p. 21; (right); © age fotostock/SuperStock, p. 22; © George Grall/National Geographic/ Getty Images, p. 23; © Heiko Kiera/Shutterstock.com, pp. 24, 29 (left); © C.C. Lockwood/Animals Animals, p. 25 (top); © iStockphoto.com/clark42, p. 25 (bottom); © Chrisp543/Dreamstime.com, p. 26; © LesPalenik/ Shutterstock.com, p. 27; © FLPA/SuperStock, p. 28; © Edwin Giesbers/naturepl.com, p. 29 (right).

Front cover: ©Donald M. Jones/Minden Pictures/Newscom.
Back cover: © Phillip Capper/flickr.com (CC BY 2.0).

Main body text set in Calvert MT Std 12/18. Typeface provided by Monotype Typography.

Library of Congress Cataloging-in-Publication Data

Hirsch, Rebecca E.
    American alligators : armored roaring reptiles / Rebecca E. Hirsch.
        pages   cm. — (Comparing animal traits)
    Includes bibliographical references.
    Audience: Ages 7–10
    Audience: Grades K to grade 3.
    ISBN 978-1-4677-7984-5 (lb : alk. paper) — ISBN 978-1-4677-8282-1 (pb : alk. paper) —
ISBN 978-1-4677-8283-8 (EB pdf)
    1. American alligator—Juvenile literature. I. Title.
QL666.C925H57   2015
597.98'4—dc23   2015001956

Manufactured in the United States of America
1 — BP — 7/15/15

TABLE OF CONTENTS

MEET THE AMERICAN ALLIGATOR

A male alligator drifts through the water in a swamp. He lifts his snout to the sky, bulges his throat, and lets out a low, rumbling roar. The sound sends ripples through the water. All around the swamp, other alligators respond with roars of their own.

American alligators spend a lot of time in the water.

American alligators are a kind of reptile, a group of animals that includes lizards, snakes, and turtles. Other animal groups are mammals, amphibians, birds, fish, and insects. Reptiles differ from these animal groups. All reptiles have three traits in common. Reptiles are vertebrates, meaning they have backbones. They have scales covering their skin. And they are cold-blooded. Their bodies don't stay the same internal temperature. Instead, reptiles soak up heat from the sun to warm their bodies. They rest in water or shade to cool their bodies. American alligators share these traits with all reptiles. But alligators also have traits that make them unique.

CHAPTER 1

WHAT DO AMERICAN ALLIGATORS LOOK LIKE?

American alligators are the largest reptiles in North America. An adult male alligator is usually about 14 to 15 feet (4.3 to 4.6 meters) long, about the length of a car. Females can reach about 10 feet (3 m) long. An American alligator has short legs and a big mouth filled with sharp teeth. An alligator has tough, scaly skin that works like armor.

DID YOU KNOW?

About **EIGHTY** teeth fill an alligator's big mouth. As the teeth wear down, new ones grow. An alligator may go through up to three thousand teeth in its lifetime!

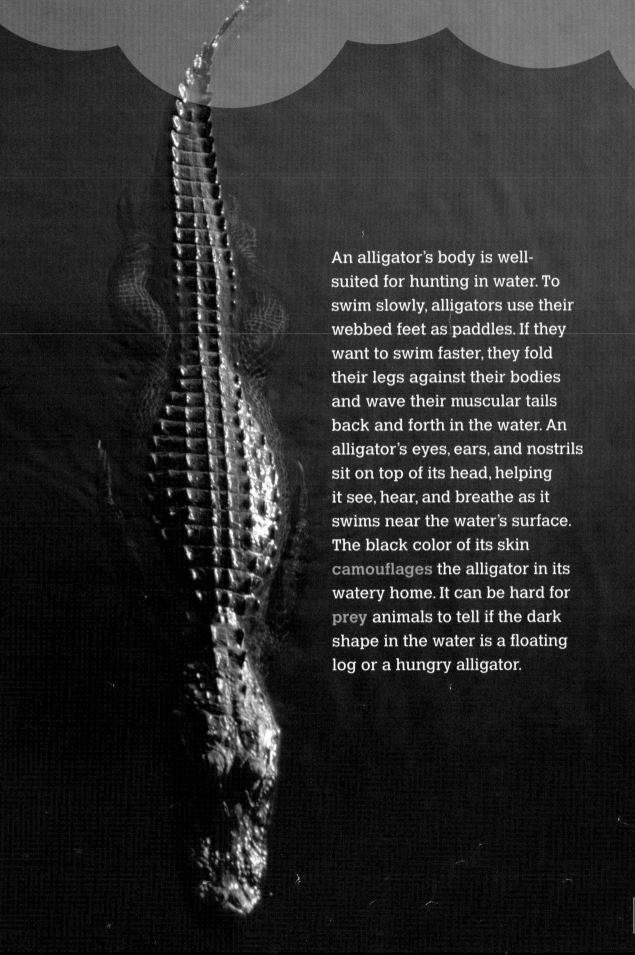

An alligator's body is well-suited for hunting in water. To swim slowly, alligators use their webbed feet as paddles. If they want to swim faster, they fold their legs against their bodies and wave their muscular tails back and forth in the water. An alligator's eyes, ears, and nostrils sit on top of its head, helping it see, hear, and breathe as it swims near the water's surface. The black color of its skin camouflages the alligator in its watery home. It can be hard for prey animals to tell if the dark shape in the water is a floating log or a hungry alligator.

AMERICAN ALLIGATORS VS. AMERICAN CROCODILES

A large American crocodile walks along a riverbank. The crocodile slips into the water without making a splash. American crocodiles and American alligators look alike in many ways. Both have lizard-like bodies with long, powerful tails. An American crocodile's grayish-green skin is lighter in color than an American alligator's skin. Both have tough, armored skin with bony scales. Both animals are usually about the same size, although American crocodiles in South America have been known to grow up to 20 feet (6.1 m) long.

American alligators and American crocodiles have eyes and ears on top of their heads and long snouts with nostrils at the tip. The snout of an alligator is wide and shaped like the letter *U*. A crocodile's snout is pointed and V-shaped. Both reptiles use their mouths full of sharp teeth for eating meat.

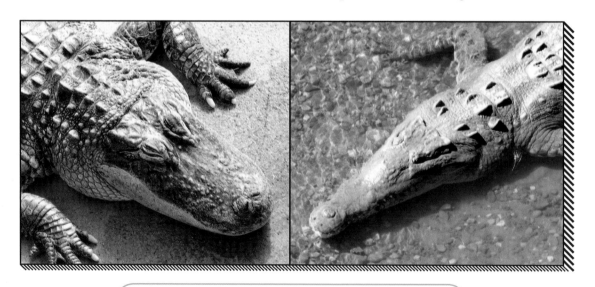

An American crocodile (*right*) has a pointed snout, and an American alligator (*left*) has a snout that is rounded.

COMPARE IT!

AMERICAN ALLIGATORS

VS.

AMERICAN CROCODILES

15 FEET
(4.6 M)

◀ MAXIMUM SIZE ▶

20 FEET
(6.1 M)

BUMPY AND ARMORED WITH BONY SCALES

◀ SKIN ▶

BUMPY AND ARMORED WITH BONY SCALES

Sharp for eating meat

◀ TEETH ▶

Sharp for eating meat

AMERICAN ALLIGATORS VS. EASTERN CORAL SNAKES

An eastern coral snake slithers along a tree branch. These brightly colored snakes live in southeastern North America. They can grow up to 30 inches (76 centimeters) long. Coral snakes look quite different from American alligators.

Unlike an American alligator, an eastern coral snake's body is slender with no arms and no legs. An American alligator has a long head with eyes on top. But a coral snake has a blunt snout, and its eyes sit on the side of its head.

An eastern coral snake has eyes on the side of its head.

Eastern coral snakes live in sandy, wooded areas.

The scaly skin of an eastern coral snake isn't black and bumpy like an American alligator's skin. The snake's skin feels smooth and has bright red, black, and yellow rings. These bright colors warn predators. They say, "Leave me alone. I am dangerous." Eastern coral snakes have sharp fangs used to inject venom.

DID YOU KNOW?
Coral snakes rarely bite people. But their bites can be **DEADLY** and must be treated quickly.

CHAPTER 2

WHERE DO AMERICAN ALLIGATORS LIVE?

American alligators live in the southeastern United States.
Most live in Florida and Louisiana. You can find them in swamps, marshes, lakes, streams, and rivers.

Alligators spend most of their time in the water. They lie motionless near the surface as they look and listen for prey. A hungry alligator will eat just about any animal it can catch. They gobble fish, turtles, snakes, birds, and small mammals.

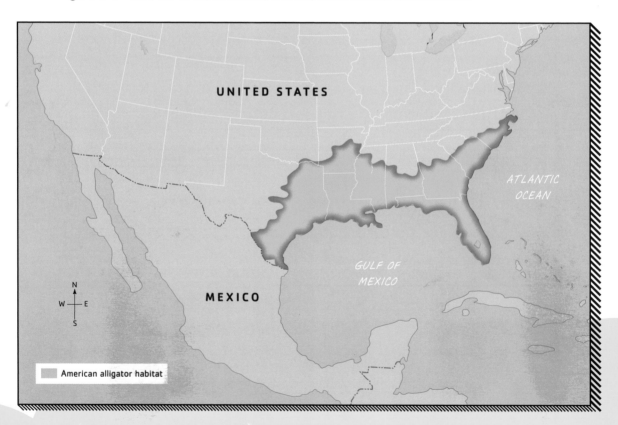

UNITED STATES

ATLANTIC OCEAN

GULF OF MEXICO

MEXICO

N
W — E
S

American alligator habitat

DID YOU KNOW?
In the past, people hunted American allligators to the edge of **EXTINCTION**. Modern laws protect alligators, and they are no longer endangered. More than one million wild alligators live in the United States.

Alligators play an important role in their habitat. On land, an alligator digs a hollow in the mud called a gator hole. In the rainy season, the gator hole fills up with water. In the dry season, as water dries up in other parts of a swamp, the deep hole stays filled with water. The hole provides a home not only for the alligator but for fish, frogs, and other animals. Birds come to the hole to eat and drink. The gator hole helps these animals survive during the dry season. The animals are usually safe near the alligator. Alligators may go days or weeks without eating.

An alligator rests in its gator hole.

AMERICAN ALLIGATORS VS. GREEN ANACONDAS

A green anaconda slides through the water of a grassy marsh. Its eyes and nostrils perch on top of its head so it can see and breathe as it swims. Green anacondas inhabit grasslands and rain forests in South America. They live in swamps, marshes, streams, and rivers. Like American alligators, anacondas hunt in the water.

Like American alligators, green anacondas live near water.

A green anaconda squeezes prey to death before eating it.

Both American alligators and green anacondas will eat just about anything that swims, flies, crawls, or walks. Green anacondas eat animals such as turtles, birds, caimans, wild pigs, deer, capybaras, and jaguars. The huge snake searches for prey as it slithers through the water with only the top of its head exposed.

DID YOU KNOW?

Green anacondas are the heaviest snakes in the world. Their bulky bodies can weigh more than **550 POUNDS** (250 kilograms)! They can grow to **30 FEET** (9.1 m) long.

AMERICAN ALLIGATORS VS. DESERT NIGHT LIZARDS

A desert night lizard scrambles over a rock. It slips into a crack and disappears from view. Desert night lizards are just 3 to 5.5 inches (7.6 to 14 cm) long from head to tail. These small reptiles live in different habitats from American alligators.

American alligators inhabit swamps, marshes, streams, and rivers. Night lizards live in deserts in the southwestern United States and northwestern Mexico. American alligators need standing water in their habitat, but night lizards don't. They drink by licking drops of moisture that collect on their bodies.

American alligators spend time swimming. Desert night lizards spend most of their time hiding. They hide in rock cracks, in rotting stumps, and under fallen leaves and tree branches. Desert night lizards seldom leave their hiding places.

A desert night lizard climbs across a rocky surface.

COMPARE IT!

AMERICAN ALLIGATORS

 **VS.**

DESERT NIGHT LIZARDS

SWAMPS, MARSHES, LAKES, STREAMS, RIVERS ◄ HABITAT ► **DESERTS**

SOUTHEASTERN UNITED STATES ◄ GEOGRAPHIC AREA ► **SOUTHWESTERN UNITED STATES AND NORTHWESTERN MEXICO**

 ◄ WHERE THEY LIVE IN THEIR HABITAT ►

In and near water

In and near rock cracks, dead plants, and other hiding places

CHAPTER 3

AMERICAN ALLIGATORS IN ACTION

An American alligator drifts quietly with the current of a river. Its body is underwater, but its eyes are above the surface, watching the shore for a meal. A bird has come to the water's edge to drink. The alligator moves closer and springs to life. It lunges forward and uses its teeth to snare the bird.

An American alligator catches a bird.

DID YOU KNOW?
On hot, sunny days, American alligators spend time on land with their big mouths open. This behavior helps **COOL** their bodies, similar to a dog panting.

Alligators spend a lot of time lying still. They hunt by remaining motionless in the water until prey is near. When an alligator attacks, it catches prey in its powerful jaws. It swallows a small animal in one gulp. It drags a large animal underwater and drowns it. If the prey is too large to swallow, the alligator tears off chunks. Sometimes an alligator spins wildly in the water, around and around like a rolling log, as it rips at the body of its prey.

Male alligators sometimes announce their presence with loud roars. A male points his head upward, takes in air, and vibrates his throat. His roar is a way to attract females and warn other males to stay away from his territory. A nearby female may also roar in response. If many alligators live close together, they may roar together in a chorus.

AMERICAN ALLIGATORS VS. FRILLED LIZARDS

A male frilled lizard is in his territory when he spies another frilled lizard. He runs to the other lizard and opens a large frill, or skin flap, around his neck. These odd-looking lizards live in woodlands in Australia and Papua New Guinea. They can grow to 3 feet (0.9 m) long from head to tail. Both frilled lizards and American alligators are predators, and they hunt in similar ways.

American alligators and frilled lizards hide and wait for their prey to come near. An alligator hides in the water. A frilled lizard stays motionless in a tree as it waits for insects, spiders, and small mammals. The lizard's grayish-brown skin makes its body look like part of the tree.

Frilled lizards don't roar the way alligators do. But they do communicate with one another and males defend their territories. Male frilled lizards flap their frills, open their mouths, and bob their heads. This behavior attracts females and warns males to stay away.

Two frilled lizards open their frills.

COMPARE IT!

AMERICAN ALLIGATORS

 VS.

FRILLED LIZARDS

FISH, TURTLES, SNAKES, BIRDS, MAMMALS

◀ **WHAT IT EATS** ▶

INSECTS, SPIDERS, SMALL MAMMALS

Remains motionless in water

◀ **HOW IT HUNTS** ▶

Remains motionless in trees

ROARS

◀ **WAY IT COMMUNICATES** ▶

OPENS ITS FRILL AND BOBS ITS HEAD

AMERICAN ALLIGATORS VS. RED-BELLIED TURTLES

A red-bellied turtle swims beneath the surface of a pond. It paddles with its front and back feet and stops to nibble on plants growing in the water. Red-bellied turtles live in lakes, rivers, ponds, and creeks in the eastern United States. The shells of these large turtles can grow to 10 to 12 inches (25 to 30 cm), about the length of a shoe box. Red-bellied turtles have different behaviors from American alligators.

A red-bellied turtle perches on a tree branch.

Red-bellied turtles often share territory with one another.

American alligators are hunters, but red-bellied turtles mostly eat plants that grow in the water. Sometimes these turtles snack on crayfish, snails, fish, and tadpoles. If an American alligator wants a meal, it lies still and waits for prey to come near. But a hungry red-bellied turtle paddles through the water and munches the food it finds.

Male American alligators defend their territory from other males. But red-bellied turtles don't mind sharing a spot. They often **bask** in groups, soaking up the sun together on a log or a rock.

CHAPTER 4

THE LIFE CYCLE OF AMERICAN ALLIGATORS

American alligators look fierce, but female alligators are attentive mothers. After a male and female alligator mate in spring, the female builds a large mound out of mud and plants near the water's edge. She chooses a spot above the water level so a flood won't destroy her eggs. She digs a hole in the top of the mound, lays about twenty to fifty eggs, and covers them. Then she stays nearby and guards the nest.

Near the end of summer, the baby alligators begin to chirp inside their eggs. The mother hears their calls and knows her babies are hatching. She digs up the nest. If there are unhatched eggs, she rolls them gently in her mouth to break the shells. Then she carries the hatchlings in her mouth to the water.

American alligators hatch near the end of summer.

A female American alligator carries a hatchling to the water.

The baby alligators stay with their mother for one to two years. Sometimes they ride on her back or in her mouth. When alligators are about ten years old, they are mature enough to mate. American alligators keep growing throughout their lives and may live for more than thirty years.

DID YOU KNOW?

Alligator hatchlings are **6 TO 8 INCHES** (15 to 20 cm) long and are black with yellow stripes. The youngsters grow quickly, about a foot (0.3 m) a year.

AMERICAN ALLIGATORS VS. CAIMANS

A female caiman walks along a riverbank and slides into the water. Several baby caimans follow behind her. Caimans live in South America and southern Mexico. They are smaller than American alligators and grow to about 8 feet (2.4 m) long. The life cycles of caimans and American alligators are quite similar.

Caiman hatchlings are around the same size as American alligator hatchlings.

After mating, a female caiman lays about twenty to forty eggs in a nest of plants and mud near the water. The mother guards the nest until she hears her babies squeak. She digs them up and leads them to the water. She may also carry them to the water in her mouth. The hatchlings are about 6 inches (15 cm) long, similar to the size of a small baby alligator.

A young caiman stays near its mother for one to two years, which is about the same amount of time that a young American alligator stays with its mother. Caimans are mature enough to mate in about seven years, a little sooner than alligators. Caimans continue to grow bigger as they grow older. It is not known how long caimans usually live in the wild. The oldest known caiman was sixty years old, but most probably survive for thirty to forty years.

AMERICAN ALLIGATORS VS. COMMON LIZARDS

A common lizard creeps through a garden. It pokes its head into the dirt and catches a spider in its jaws. Adult common lizards are just 2 to 3 inches (5.1 to 7.6 cm) long. You can find these small reptiles across Europe and northern Asia. Common lizards have very different life cycles than American alligators.

All alligators lay eggs, as do most reptiles. A few reptiles give birth to live young instead. But some common lizards lay eggs, while others give birth. In northern parts of their range, female common lizards lay eggs. To the south, they give birth to live young. Scientists are not sure why common lizards reproduce differently depending on where they live, although it may help the young lizards survive in different habitats.

Young common lizards don't receive any care from their mothers. They are on their own as soon as they are hatched or born. The lizards are ready to mate in only two years, much sooner than American alligators. Common lizards live about five years, compared to more than thirty years for alligators.

COMPARE IT!

AMERICAN ALLIGATORS

VS.

COMMON LIZARDS

	HOW THEY REPRODUCE	
Lay eggs	◄ ►	Lay eggs or give birth to live young

	CARE FROM MOTHER AFTER HATCHING/ BIRTH	
PROTECT YOUNG FOR 1 TO 2 YEARS	◄ ►	**NONE**

	TYPICAL LIFE SPAN	
MORE THAN 30 YEARS	◄ ►	**5 YEARS**

AMERICAN ALLIGATORS TRAIT CHART

This book explores the ways American alligators are similar to and different from other reptiles. What favorite reptiles would you add to this list?

	COLD-BLOODED	SCALES ON BODY	LAYS EGGS	LONG SNOUT	HUNTS IN WATER	CARNIVORE
AMERICAN ALLIGATOR	X	X	X	X	X	X
AMERICAN CROCODILE	X	X	X	X	X	X
EASTERN CORAL SNAKE	X	X	X			X
GREEN ANACONDA	X	X			X	X
DESERT NIGHT LIZARD	X	X				X
FRILLED LIZARD	X	X	X			X
RED-BELLIED TURTLE	X	X	X		X	
CAIMAN	X	X	X	X	X	X
COMMON LIZARD	X	X	X*			X

*SOME GIVE BIRTH

GLOSSARY

bask: to lie or rest in a warm place

caimans: South American reptiles that are closely related to alligators

camouflages: covers up or changes the way an animal looks to make it easier to hide from prey and predators

capybaras: South American rodents often exceeding 4 feet (1.2 m) long. They are usually found in or near water.

communicate: to transmit information to other animals using sound, sight, touch, taste, or smell. Animals communicate to attract mates, warn off predators, and identify themselves.

fierce: eager to fight or kill

habitat: an environment where an animal naturally lives. A habitat is the place where an animal can find food, water, air, shelter, and a place to raise its young.

hatchlings: recently hatched animals

predators: animals that hunt, or prey on, other animals

prey: an animal that is hunted and killed by a predator for food

range: the area where a certain kind of animal lives

reproduce: to create offspring

territory: an area that is occupied and defended by an animal or a group of animals

traits: features that are inherited from parents. Body size and skin color are examples of inherited traits.

venom: poison produced by some snakes and passed to a victim by biting

SELECTED BIBLIOGRAPHY

"American Alligator: *Alligator mississippiensis*." US Fish & Wildlife Service. Accessed December 5, 2014. http://www.fws.gov/endangered/esa -library/pdf/alligator.pdf.

"American Alligator: Species Profile." National Park Service. Accessed December 3, 2014. http://www.nps.gov /ever/naturescience/alligator.htm.

"Animals." *National Geographic*. Accessed September 8, 2014. http://animals .nationalgeographic.com/animals/.

Halliday, Tim, and Kraig Adler. *Firefly Encyclopedia of Reptiles and Amphibians*. Toronto: Firefly Books, 2002.

FURTHER INFORMATION

Heos, Bridget. *What to Expect When You're Expecting Hatchlings: A Guide for Crocodilian Parents (and Curious Kids)*. Minneapolis: Millbrook Press, 2012. Open this book for a humorous take on the life cycles of alligators and other crocodilians.

McCarthy, Colin. *Reptile*. New York: DK, 2012. Check out this book to discover more about alligators and many kinds of reptiles.

National Geographic—Alligators' Hunting Secrets Revealed by Crittercams http://news.nationalgeographic.com /news/2014/01/140115-alligator -crittercam-hunting-animals-behavior -science
Watch alligators hunt from their point of view.

San Diego Zoo Animals—Crocodilian http://animals.sandiegozoo.org/animals /crocodilian
Learn with photos and quick facts about crocodilians.

INDEX